Cryptocurrency

A Beginner's Guide To Understanding And Winning With Fintech (Bitcoin, Blockchain, Trading, Investing, Mining, Digital Money, Smart Contracts)

Eliot P. Reznor

Cryptocurrency: A Beginner's Guide To Understanding And Winning With Fintech (Bitcoin, Blockchain, Trading, Investing, Mining, Digital Money, Smart Contracts)

Table of Contents

1 - Introduction

Thank you for taking the time to buy this book. This book will serve as your guide in exploring the exciting opportunities and risks in the world of cryptocurrencies. Learning is crucial if you want to succeed in any endeavor, and this is true when it comes to cryptocurrencies, which is regarded as the future cash of the world.

Through this book, you will be able to learn the following:

- The origins of cryptocurrencies and why it is now becoming popular among non-technical users

- The Blockchain technology and why it is considered as a breakthrough innovation in the world of financial technology

- The pros and cons of using digital currencies

- The top cryptocurrencies according to popularity, value, and market capitalization

- How you can make money in cryptocurrency

- The future outlook of cryptocurrency – Is it a fad or a breakthrough technology?

1 - INTRODUCTION

Once again, thanks for buying this book, I hope you find it to be helpful!

2 - What Is Cryptocurrency

A cryptocurrency is a currency in virtual or digital form, which utilizes cryptographic technology to add security to process transfer and safekeeping. Because of this security feature, a cryptocurrency can be difficult to counterfeit.

Its organic nature is a distinctive feature of a cryptocurrency and usually regarded as its best feature. No central authority releases cryptocurrency, so in theory, it cannot be subjected to government manipulation or interference.

Early Days of Cryptocurrency

Although Bitcoin, arguably the most popular cryptocurrency today, was only introduced in 2008, the first recorded attempt in using a virtual form of cash was during the late 1980s. In the Netherlands, gas stations in the rural areas were often robbed. Obviously, the owners were not happy with the circumstances as they need to operate day and night so lorries can refuel.

One suggested the idea of loading money into smart cards, which was then being tested out. It was the beginning of electronic cash. Truck drivers were provided with these cards instead of cash, and so the incidence of robbery went down.

During the same time, Albert Heijn (a major retailer in Netherlands) was lobbying for banks to come up with a system that will allow consumers to directly pay from their bank accounts, which later developed as Point of Sale or POS.

Virtual Cash

Meanwhile in the US, a Cryptographer David Chaum had been working on a system that will use virtual cash. His research on currency and privacy caused him to believe that to be able to do business safely, there is a need for a currency that will mimic the purpose of actual bank notes and coins.

In particular, Chaum is looking into the capacity of a system that will allow anyone to pay safely and privately without the interference of a third party such as a bank.

David Chaum created an extension of the RSA algorithm, which is now being used in encrypting data in the web. This blinding formula enables anyone to transfer a number to anyone, and this number is subject to modification by the receiver. Once the receiver keeps the coin into the bank, it still has the authentic signature of the mint. However, this is not the same number that the mint has signed.

This system allowed the coin to be changed without a trace and without damaging the original signature of the mint. Therefore, the bank or the mint is blind to the process. This interest, as well as more favorable policies on privacy, persuaded Chaum to live in Netherlands.

He worked with the CWI, which was a bastion for mathematical research and cryptography. During his tenure at CWI, he created DigiCash and led to the creation of virtual money. He mentored other cryptographers and pioneers in cryptocurrency including Bryce Wilcox-Ahearn, Nick Szabo, Marcel Van Der Peijl, Gary Howland, Niels Ferguson, and Stefan Brands.

The invention of virtual cash caused a frenzy and it has caught a lot of attention from the public. However, David Chaum and his team made some misfortunes and experienced some entanglements with the Central Bank of Netherlands or the DNB.

It turned out that Chaum agreed that the virtual cash will only be offered to the banks. This arrangement then caused the company to offer the virtual cash through numerous banks, which led to the company's bankruptcy in 1998.

The feverish attention in the press attracted potential big deals such as Deutsche Bank and Microsoft, but Chaum failed to take advantage to propel. It was even reported that Microsoft offered as much as $180 million to Chaum so that every Windows PC will be enabled with DigiCash. Chaum thought the offer was not enough, and so Microsoft backed down, and Chaum went bankrupt.

Online Cash

Despite Chaum's bankruptcy, DigiCash was a breakthrough invention, and in fact, on its coattails, many startups were created to work on this area. During the 1990s, the interest in virtual cash increased in the USA primarily because Europe has implemented regulatory policies on digital cash. Meanwhile, in the US, Netscape had just launched its IPO.

However, the first wave of using cryptocurrency immediately faded and was replaced by the second wave of online cash. The first wave of excitement was First Virtual, which was the predecessor of PayPal. While First Virtual was strict on its policy of being a merchant before accepting money, PayPal allowed cash to be transferred from one person to another.

Hence, PayPal became more popular than First Virtual who acted like regular banks. PayPal also introduced some innovations such as its system of literally handing cash via the Palm Pilot, which was very popular among geeks.

This focus on geeks, was immediately abandoned as the company realized that majority of its users are really looking for a way to send and receive money through the internet. It also secured a large consumer base within the eBay community, so PayPal propelled to great heights.

This popularity has proven that online can become a protocol of choice, even for financial transactions. Hence, the ideas of Chaum were nevertheless used but largely forgotten in North America. However, Chaum's system was still thriving in Russia through the use of WebMoney. Several startups were also established to work on harnessing money through the web.

E-gold was a company that initially succeeded in this field. Its operation was based in the US, but it was registered as a corporation in the Caribbean. This company offers a very easy system - a client sends in precious metals such as gold or silver, and the company will credit e-gold to his account. The client can also purchase new e-gold by sending a wire to the company, which will buy and keep the physical gold.

The company became popular among gold traders and investors. Because the company was based in the Caribbean, there is no need for the US government to approve the process. The system enticed the American market for goldbugs as well as the increasingly global community of online traders who need to facilitate international payments.

As you might even guess, e-gold was then subjected to a government investigation, mainly because of the system's policy of allowing anyone to sign up for an account. Even though this is not illegal, the increasing incidence of online scams caught the attention of FBI.

The Feds raided the company's office in Florida, which has cracked down its operation and caused the downfall of e-gold as an online currency. Also, FBI winded up similar companies, which ensured the end of the second wave of the new currency.

Before the events of the September 11 attacks, the US was quite liberal about allowing alternative currencies. The US government saw the potential of an alternative currency for business and innovation. But after September 11, this perception dramatically changed.

Cryptocurrencies were perceived to be the platform for facilitating transactions to fund drug deals and terrorist activities. Hence, cryptocurrencies were targeted for control.

Bitcoin

Before the Nixon Shock, the US dollar has been based on the amount of gold that the US Treasury holds. Practically, you can exchange your dollars for its value in gold. In comparison, cryptocurrencies such as Bitcoin, are not based on gold or silver but based on mathematical mints.

Bitcoins are created using a sophisticated layer of mathematical formula, which runs on computers. The network has access to a public ledger through Blockchain technology which records and confirms every processed transaction.

A single entity like the central bank cannot control the Bitcoin ledger. The primary concept of Bitcoin is decentralization, which refers to the independent nature of the transaction from the interference of manipulation of a government, a country, or a bank.

But who created Bitcoin? Well, there is no clear answer to this as the popular name of the creator is still shrouded in mystery. The publisher of the whitepaper describing Bitcoin and the use of Blockchain system is just a nome de plume - Satoshi Nakamoto. His Blockchain account is no longer active, and even the BTC in his wallet was never spent.

However, some people believe that Satoshi Nakamoto refers to the group of people who are experts in cryptocurrency including Charles Bry, Vladimir Oksman, and Neal King. This group actually filed for a patent for the Bitcoin before the Bitcoin domain was purchased. This is very far from a mere coincidence.

On October 31, 2008, a whitepaper was published describing the foundation of the Bitcoin system. It was entitled "Bitcoin: A Peer-to-Peer Electronic Cash System" was published to a cryptography mailing list. The author was listed as Satoshi Nakamoto.

However, it was two months prior to this publication that the Bitcoin.org was purchased specifically on August 18, 2008. The prototype version of Bitcoin was only announced on January 8, 2009, and it began the frenzy for Bitcoin mining.

It is just fitting that the creator of Bitcoin hides its real identity, as privacy is a key concern for Bitcoin and its users. While it is still unknown who created Bitcoin, it is a fact that this breakthrough technology has started a revolution in the financial world.

3 - How Cryptocurrency Works?

As the name suggests, cryptocurrencies are currencies that are encrypted in code. As a currency, it can be transmitted from one person to another and verified in a public ledger through a mining process.

In this Chapter, we will take a general overview of how cryptocurrencies such as Bitcoin work. We first need to go over the basics of cryptocurrency, and then we will also cover the other important features of common cryptocurrencies today.

Basic Concepts of Cryptocurrency

To fully understand the mechanism behind cryptocurrencies, it is important to understand first some basic concepts: public ledgers, transactions, and mining.

Public Ledger

In cryptocurrency, a public ledger is used to store all verified transaction from the creation of a cryptocurrency. When you use a cryptocurrency, your identity will be encrypted, and the system will use other encryption techniques to make certain that the record keeping will be accurate.

The public ledger ensures that the specific digital wallet could calculate the correct available amount. In addition, new currency transactions could be verified to ensure that every transaction only uses coins that are owned by a certain identity. In Bitcoin, this public ledger is known as a Blockchain.

Transactions

Similar to a bank transaction, a transaction in cryptocurrency refers to the transmission of cryptocurrency from one owner of a digital wallet to another. This transaction is filed into the public ledger for verification.

Once there is a transaction, digital wallets use an encryption to bestow a mathematical code that the transaction originates from a specific owner of a wallet. The verification process may take a bit of time (about 10 minutes) for BTC while the network verifies the transaction and file them to the ledger.

Mining

In cryptocurrency, mining refers to the process of verifying the transaction and linking them to the public ledger. To link a transaction to the public ledger, a miner should be able to solve a mathematical problem. In Bitcoin, mining is open source, so anyone could verify any transaction. The first miner who will solve the mathematical puzzle can link a block to the ledger.

The manner in which the transactions, processes, and the ledger work together assure that no single person could easily add or modify a block. When a block is linked to the ledger, all related transactions become permanent and a minimal transaction fee will be added to the wallet of the miner alongside the newly generated coins. The mining process provides value to the coin.

How Bitcoin Works

Arguably, the most popular cryptocurrency today is Bitcoin, and to understand how Bitcoin works, we can understand how a cryptocurrency works.

3 - HOW CRYPTOCURRENCY WORKS?

The whole Bitcoin system runs on a Peer-to-Peer or P2P network, which is similar to file-sharing networks similar to the ones, which allow people to easily transfer various forms of data, which includes pictures, music, videos, and more. Basically, a P2P system is a resilient platform.

Hence, there is no central hub that runs all Bitcoin transactions. Rather, every computer of a Bitcoin user is a part of the network, which collectively shares the load of generating the digital currency and recording their transactions. This decentralized feature makes Bitcoin free from government interference.

Bitcoins should be mined first before you can use them. Any computer can start Bitcoin mining by using a free mining application. This requires the whole network of computers to perform a set of work before getting bitcoins as a reward.

In general, this work entails several computers solving mathematical problems, and the rewards will be given to the owner of the PC, which completes the calculation at hand. Hence, it is not surprising that some people have decided to invest in super powerful computers for bitcoin mining.

The specific amount of work needed is variable. The network can adjust the workload so that the number of bitcoins will increase at a stable and predetermined number. This will continue to perform until it reaches 21 million, which is the maximum number of bitcoins in circulation.

At present, the mining process could generate 25 bitcoins every 10 minutes. And every four years will be decreased by 50% until the maximum limit of Bitcoins will be achieved. This is projected to happen in the year 2140. After this, the circulation of Bitcoin will be static.

You have to keep your bitcoins in your digital wallet. If you receive or send bitcoins, they will be validated by a digital signature, which is known as an encryption key that safeguards the currency from counterfeits. The network keeps the whole transaction in a public ledger known as Blockchain, which is a safe way to monitor the circulation of bitcoins.

This is possible thanks to the open-source nature of Bitcoin. As a short background, the principle of open source software is often used by programmers who are against corporate control and profiteering.

Hence, any experienced programmer can see how the programming behind the system is working. Non-programmers may think that this is a threat to the security of the network, but this is actually an ingenious way for the whole network to confirm the legitimacy for every transfer.

Bitcoin as a Cryptocurrency

Similar to any currency, you can keep your Bitcoins in your account, and hopefully they appreciate in value. You can also cash them out and convert into your preferred traditional currency. If you choose to keep them on your computer, it is important to take note that there is no central network that will serve as a backup for your data stored in your wallet.

Therefore, you should keep your own record of bitcoins. It is recommended to keep this record on a device like a flash drive, which you can keep away in a safe location. You might lose all your record of bitcoin savings if you lose your laptop or your computer crashes down.

You can never reverse a Bitcoin transaction, and it is quite fast to complete. But because the verification process for

3 - HOW CRYPTOCURRENCY WORKS?

Bitcoin transaction requires data sharing with the whole network, there are times that you have to wait for a few minutes before you can complete payment.

Because Bitcoin is not regulated by any government, it is easy to transfer them to any point of the globe and without paying the high fees that banks usually charge for overseas transactions. And with the absence of a governing body, your Bitcoin account has no restrictions, and can never be subjected to a free order.

This sounds too good to be true, and in fact, many people are questioning the legitimacy of cryptocurrencies. It seems dubious that a currency can just appear in a few minutes online and have real value. We can discuss here the comprehensive and philosophical basis of money, but we can sum up the essence of currency with this - all currencies are valuable because people agreed to believe that they have value.

People who use Bitcoin trust the encryption and mathematics of the whole system, and this trust has been cultivated through the years, and similar to any currency, has been accepted by a large community.

Current Worth of Bitcoin

As of May 2017, 1 BTC is equivalent to $1,223, which is a significant jump from its value in 2016 when it was only about $ 770 on average. The price of Bitcoin is also dependent on the volume of mining processes, because of more mining activities, the more it becomes difficult and so more expensive to generate new coins.

Therefore, the price of Bitcoin should increase as the production cost also increases. The aggregate power of the mining network of Bitcoin has increased to threefold over the past year.

How Bitcoin Mining Works?

Bitcoin transactions happen all the time, and without a way to keep all these transactions, there is no way to monitor who has paid what. This is being taken care of the Bitcoin network by collecting all the transactions that have occurred during a specific period in the list known as the block. It is the role of the miner to verify these transactions and add them to the public ledger.

This public ledger is basically a long list of blocks called the Blockchain. This could be used to explore any transaction made between Bitcoin users and at any point in the system.

If the system creates a new block, it will be added to the chain, which creates the whole list of all the transactions that happened in the network. Because the ledger is public, everyone who participates in the network can access the transactions.

However, a general ledger should be trusted, and it should be kept in a digital format. This is an area of concern because it could be difficult to be certain that the Blockchain remains solid and untampered. This is the reason why the role of Bitcoin miners is important.

Once a block of transactions is generated, Bitcoin miners verify the process. They read the information in the block, and use a certain mathematical formula, which converts it into another code. This code is known as a hash, which is simply a random sequence of numbers and letters. This hash is kept along with the block, at the end of the Blockchain at any given time.

3 - HOW CRYPTOCURRENCY WORKS?

It can be easy to generate a hash from a group of data such as a Bitcoin block. However, it can be quite impossible to read the data just by looking at the hash. And although it can be easy to generate a hash from a large group of data, every data is one of a kind. The hash will be completely changed if you change just one character in a block.

Bitcoin miners are not just using the transactions in a block to create a hash. Other forms of data are also used, which includes the hash of the last stored block in the chain.

In a way, this becomes an electronic version of a wax seal because the hash of each block is generated using the hash of the prior block. This verifies that this block, as well as the block after it - is genuine because everyone will notice if the block has been tampered.

If a user attempts to tamper a transaction by changing a block, which has already been linked into the chain, the hash of this block will change. If one user verifies the authenticity of the block by taking a look at the hash, he will find that the hash doesn't align with the one already linked with the block. Hence, this block will be immediately flagged as tampered.

Because every hash of the block is used to help in creating the hash of the next block in the chain, changing the block will also make the next block misaligned, too. This will continue all the way down, which will throw the whole chain in a chaos.

This is how miners verify the block. They are all in a competition to perform the seal off through the help of software that is programmed particularly for block mining. Each time a user successfully generates a hash, he receives 25 Bitcoins, the system will update the block, and every participant in the network will be notified. This is the main motivation to keep mining and keep the transactions happening.

The main concern is that it can be easy to generate a hash from a data group, as computers are very powerful nowadays. As a response, the Bitcoin network should make it more difficult to do this, or else anyone will be able to hash thousands of bitcoins every minute, and the currency will be ubiquitous.

The special protocol used by Bitcoin makes it extra difficult to mine the currency by requiring proof of work.

This protocol will not accept any old hash. It requires that a has a certain block should look a specific way. It should have a specific number of zeroes at the beginning. You just can't tell what a hash will look like before you generate it, and when you introduce a new piece of data in the chain, the hash will be changed.

Miners are not allowed to interfere with the block's data transaction, but they should modify the data that they are using to generate a specific hash. This is possible by using a random piece of data known as nonce, which is used with the system to generate a hash.

When the hash does not fit the required format, the nonce will be changed, and the entire system will be hashed again. The user may take several attempts to search for a nonce that works and all the miners are performing this task simultaneously. This is how you can earn bitcoins through mining.

Getting a Bitcoin Wallet

Just like other currencies, you need to have a method to keep your cryptocurrencies. When it comes to Bitcoins, you have to have a digital wallet, which actually behaves a lot more like a bank account.

Different wallets offer different levels of security depending on the security level you prefer. Some wallets can be used like daily spending accounts and can be best compared to the actual physical wallet while other wallets are protected with military-grade encryption as they may contain Bitcoins that are worth millions of dollars.

There are three primary options when it comes to digital wallets:

- A web-based online service

- A digital wallet kept on the hard drive of your PC

- Vault service, which stores the Bitcoins or a multi-signature wallet using a number of codes to safeguard the account

Digital wallets have their vulnerabilities. When you keep a cryptocurrency locally on your hard drive, you need to ensure that you regularly backup your data so you can still access your record if your drive crashes down. Digital wallets also use different levels of degrees to security against hackers from minimal security (username and password) to maximum security (multi-factor authentication).

Cryptocurrency Transactions

There are also different types of transactions involving cryptocurrencies. Some are basic transactions such as a usual trade for online services while others involve hundreds of thousands of Bitcoins for corporate trading. Most wallets and exchanges will keep the amounts of cryptocurrency for the user, much like a conventional bank account.

4 - What Makes Cryptocurrencies Different

Even though there are certain exceptions, there are several factors that make cryptocurrencies quite different from the current financial systems:

Value

As you have already learned earlier, a currency is genuine if it has an agreed value. Any currency such as the Euro represents value because Europeans agree that a piece of special paper has value. This is the same principle followed by cryptocurrencies.

We have learned that the value of cryptocurrencies, such as Bitcoins, is created by miners, who are people who are running programs on their computers to solve mathematical problems. The work behind mining digital currencies provides them value, while the fluctuating demand and supply cause the value to fluctuate.

Again, the concept of work providing value to a currency is known as a proof of work approach, which is also known as proof of stake in other forms of digital currencies. Value is generated when transactions are linked to the public ledger as generating a confirmed block also requires work.

Pseudonymity

Cryptocurrency owners store their digital money in a protected wallet. The identification of the coin holder will be stored in an encrypted location, which they can control, but not linked to the identity of the person.

The link between the user and the digital currency is pseudonymous instead of anonymous because ledgers can be accessed by the public, and so these ledgers could be used to get more information about groups of people in the system.

Proof of Work

Many forms of cryptocurrencies today are using proof of work model, which uses a complicated calculation but easy to confirm mathematical problem to restrict the use of cryptocurrency mining. Basically, this is a complicated captcha, which needs high-level computational capacity.

Open Source

Cryptocurrencies are usually open source, which means that anyone can create APIs for free and can participate in the network.

Digital

Conventional currency is defined by an actual object to represent value (USD, EUR, JPY), but cryptocurrencies are all digital. Digital currencies are kept in digital wallets and can be transferred digitally to other wallets. For example, there is no physical object that represents Bitcoin.

Decentralized

The currencies that are in circulation are under control of a central government through its central bank, and so their production could be regulated by a third party. The creation and transaction involving cryptocurrencies are controlled by code, open source, and depends on the P2P network. No single authority could interfere in cryptocurrencies.

Cryptographic

Encryption is a primary feature of cryptocurrency. This is used to control the production of the digital currency and to confirm transactions.

Adaptive Scaling

Basically, cryptocurrencies are produced with a number of factors to make certain that they can work well regardless of the volume of transaction.

For example, Bitcoin is designed to permit for a single block transaction to be mined in 10-minute intervals. The algorithm adapts after 2016 blocks, which is about 2 weeks to make the mining more difficult or easier depending on the time that it took for the blocks to be mined.

The mining is easy if it only takes 10 days to mine the 2016 blocks. Therefore, the system will increase the difficulty. The difficulty will decrease if it takes more than 15 days to mine the 2016 blocks.

Several other measures are integrated into cryptocurrencies to permit adaptive scaling, which includes decreasing the reward for mining as more currencies are mined and creating scarcity by restricting the supply over time.

Don't worry if at this point you are still a bit confused on how cryptocurrencies work. It can be a real challenge to wrap your head around the basic concepts of cryptocurrencies. These concepts may be easy for some, while for others, may require a different way of discussion.

The technique with cryptocurrencies is not to be worried if you are not understanding them first. Every chapter in this book will help you learn more about cryptocurrencies until you develop a natural appreciation for them and eventually use them.

5 - Advantages and Disadvantages of Using Cryptocurrencies

After learning how cryptocurrencies work, it is ideal to learn more about the advantages and disadvantages of using a digital currency. There are several advantages that make cryptocurrency better than the traditional currencies today. However, this is still far from being perfect, so most cryptocurrencies also have their flaws. We will explore the pros and cons of cryptocurrencies in this chapter.

Advantages of Cryptocurrencies

More Freedom

With cryptocurrencies, it is easy to send and receive money anytime and anywhere you are. There is no need to worry about exchange rates, scheduling transfers to consider bank holidays or other restrictions we usually encounter when we transfer money. You can control your own money with cryptocurrencies as there is no central governing authority that will interfere with the transactions.

Let's take a look at one real example of how a digital currency works without interference from the government.

Today, there is a self-imposed crisis in Venezuela. There is a scarcity of goods in the country, while black markets are rampant. Money is also scarce, and some people have turned to using cryptocurrencies, primarily Bitcoin in order to survive.

The government subsidizes electricity, which has provided some people to earn income through Bitcoin mining. Venezuelans are using Bitcoins to purchase food from online merchants outside the country without going through the usual customs process that will take months. This is a good example on how people can use cryptocurrency for survival.

Security and Control

Without a single entity controlling all transactions, and instead allowing people to be in control of their own transactions, the system used in cryptocurrencies become inherently safe. Online merchants will not be able to charge add-on fees without prior notice to the customer.

Meanwhile, payments in cryptocurrencies could be made and verified without providing personal information to the transaction. Because of the fact that personal details are kept concealed, identity theft can be averted.

Security is a major feature that makes cryptocurrencies attractive to consumers. If you choose to pay using a credit card, you have to provide your personal information before you can purchase something online.

Likewise, if you need to send money through a wire, you also have to provide all the information that could also be used by frauds to pretend to be you and send money to anyone. Exchange of personal information is absent in dealing with cryptocurrencies, which increases security.

Transparency

The unique feature of cryptocurrencies such as Bitcoin is that it is anonymous yet transparent. Through the public ledger, all completed transactions can be accessed by anyone, yet personal details are concealed. The user's public address is visible for everyone but personal details are not included.

Cryptocurrencies work with great levels of transparency. All transactions involving a digital currency are publicly access-ible, highly traceable, and stored permanently in the ledger. Public addresses are the only details used to define the al-locations of bitcoins and where they are sent.

These addresses are privately created through individual di-gital wallets. But when addresses are already used, they are marked with all the records of all transactions they are in-volved with. Anyone in the network could access the bal-ance as well as transactions of any user.

Because users often have to reveal their personal details be-fore getting services or goods, the addresses used in crypto-currencies cannot be completely anonymous. Remember, the public ledger is permanent, so all transactions can be traced. Hence, public addresses are often used once, and users are always cautious not to reveal their addresses.

One beneficiary of the transparency offered by cryptocur-rencies is in the area of charity. Digital currencies are seen now as the solution for more transparency among charit-able organizations, specifically on how they are spending donations.

5 - ADVANTAGES AND DISADVANTAGES OF USING CRYPTOCURRENCIES

Because of the transparent mechanism of digital currencies, every transaction is unique and can be traced. Hence, it can be easy for donors to see precisely how the organization is spending their money. There are even proposals about creating a social currency that can be used only for projects for charitable causes.

Experts also hail the advantages of digital currencies when it comes to donating funds overseas as it can considerably decrease the costs of currency trading when transferring money from one country to another. Charities can also tap into individuals and companies who have made a sizable fortune via these online currencies.

Affordable Fees

There are very minimal fees, and even no fees at all, in most cryptocurrency systems. For merchant transactions, both parties may agree on a specific amount of fee to expedite the process. Including a fee in the transaction will give more priority to the confirmation request so it will be processed faster.

Meanwhile, digital currency exchanges are important in

merchant transactions by trading cryptocurrency into conventional currency. In general, these services have lower fees compared to online bank transfers or through PayPal.

For instance, in Bitcoin, the transaction fee goes to the miner. Once a new block is created with a verified hash, the information for all the transaction will be included in the block and all transaction fees will be received by the miner who created the block.

The transaction fees in Bitcoin are voluntary, as you can still initiate a transaction even without adding a fee. In contrast, miners are also not required to accept the transactions and add them to the newly created block. Therefore, the transaction fee is just a small reward in the system to ensure that a certain transaction will be added to the next block.

Fewer Risks Involved for Merchant Transactions

Because of the fact that the transactions involving cryptocurrencies are mostly irreversible, and they are not linked to any personal details of the sender, merchants are safeguarded from possible losses that may arise due to fraud.

By using cryptocurrencies, online entrepreneurs can still do business in areas where fraud cases are high. This is due to the reason that it can be nearly impossible to cheat the system because of public record keeping and transparency.

Disadvantages of Cryptocurrencies

After exploring the basic advantages, let us now discuss the disadvantages of using cryptocurrencies:

Not Yet Widely Popular

Only very few people know the existence of cryptocurrencies, and not all of them are embracing its uses. Hence, it is a bit difficult to look for merchants who are accepting Bitcoins as payment for goods and services.

More and more businesses are accepting digital currencies because of their advantages, but the number is still a thin slice compared to businesses who prefer accepting cash or payment through credit cards.

There is still a need for people to be educated about cryptocurrencies and how they can use it in everyday living. In businesses that are accepting digital currencies, not all staff are knowledgeable enough of how these new currencies work, so there is also limit on how they can help their customers understand this area.

Workers should be educated on digital currency so that they could help their customers. This will, of course, require investment on the part of the business, but it will position the organization towards the potential commodity of the future.

Volatility

Digital currencies are volatile primarily because of the fact that there is still a limit on a number of currencies in circulation while the demand increases every day. But it is projected by experts that the volatility will decrease as time passes by. The price of digital currencies is expected to settle down as more businesses start accepting digital currencies, mainly Bitcoin.

In the traditional markets, volatility is measured by the Volatility Index. In digital currencies, volatility is not yet widely accepted since they are still in early stages. But it is a fact that Bitcoin is volatile in price compared to the US dollar.

At the moment, the price of digital currencies is influenced by the events related to this field. For example, the rate of adoption can be influenced by bad news, which includes the possible regulation by governments. Other significant new includes the controversial use of digital currencies in the drug trade in Silk Road as well as the bankruptcy of Mt. Gox in 2014.

The ensuing public panic caused the value of digital currencies to fall down rapidly versus the value of fiat currencies. In general, volatility is seen by experts as an indication that the market is progressing.

A reason why digital currencies fluctuate against conventional currencies is the conceived of value in comparison to fiat currency. Some properties of digital currencies such as Bitcoin are similar to gold.

For example, the amount of Bitcoin is fixed at 21 million BTC. Some people may choose to invest in digital currencies instead of fiat currencies since the latter is governed by governments who like to keep inflation at low, create more jobs and pose strong growth through capital resources investment.

The volatility of digital currencies is also influenced significantly by different perceptions of its intrinsic value as the method of value transfer and as a store of value. A method of value transfer refers to concept or object used to transfer property in the asset from one party to another. On the other hand, a store of value refers to the purpose of an asset to be used in the future.

The property could be saved and traded if the user deems necessary. The current volatility of digital currencies makes it an unlikely store of value. However, it offers easy transfer of value. Because these two factors influence the present spot price of digital currencies, their value could easily change according to news events similar to conventional currencies.

Still In Infancy Stage

Although gaining ground in the financial markets, digital currencies are still in its very early phase with developing features that are still very unstable. To ensure that the digital currency is secure and accessible, new services, tools, and features should be developed by the network and its supporters.

Digital currencies are still viable for growth before we can see its full function. Similar to any currency on its infancy stage, digital currencies are just starting out and should work out some areas of concern before it becomes widely accepted.

At this point, we now have explored the advantages and disadvantages of digital currencies. As you can see, cryptocurrencies, regardless of their breakthrough benefits in comparison with fiat currencies, are still not perfect. They have numerous benefits that conventional currencies cannot and may not even provide.

This is mostly because of the fact that they are still quite young and considered as a new currency. People are just starting to become aware and understand digital currencies. For its success, people should widely use them in their daily transactions.

5 - ADVANTAGES AND DISADVANTAGES OF USING CRYPTOCURRENCIES

There are always two sides of the coin. In order to understand and decide whether you want to use digital currencies or not, it is crucial to weigh both sides before you make your choice. Cryptocurrencies are breakthrough innovation, and it can be beneficial if you understand how it works and takes advantage of the early opportunity for investments and trading.

6 - Top Cryptocurrencies Aside from Bitcoin

The concept of cryptocurrencies has inspired many individuals and organizations to create their own form of digital currencies. Bitcoin is arguably the most popular digital currency today, but as of July 2016, there are more than 710 cryptocurrencies available in the market for trade and investment. However, only a few became successful to achieve $ 10 million market capitalization.

In this Chapter, we will explore the top cryptocurrencies available today. There is a separate chapter that explores Bitcoin, so we will cover here other digital currencies.

Ethereum (ETH)

Basically, Ethereum is an open platform that uses Blockchain technology, which enables developers to generate and use computer programs. Similar to Bitcoin, Ethereum is also a distributed public Blockchain network.

Even though there are some major technical differences between these two platforms, the most significant feature is that these two cryptocurrencies are substantially different when it comes to capacity and purpose.

Bitcoin provides one specific application of Blockchain technology - a P2P digital currency system, which enables online payments. While the Blockchain used in Bitcoin is used to monitor ownership of online cash, the Blockchain used in Ethereum is used to run codes of any decentralized app.

In Bitcoin, you have to mine to earn coins. In Ethereum, you have to work in order to earn Ether, which is a form of cryptocurrency, which fuels the system. Currently, Ether is a tradable cryptocurrency and can be used by app developers to pay for fees and services within the network.

Like most digital currencies, Ethereum is based on a P2P network, which any programmer can use to run Dapps or distributed applications. The network can run any computer program, but the network is designed to perform rules, which are executed if specific conditions are present similar to a contract. The Ethereum network uses its own public ledger to store, run, and secure these contracts.

Every computer on the network installs a small virtual machine that will sync with the Blockchain and remains accessible to enforce contracts. The computer network easily provides the reliability, computing capacity, and security needed to perform the stipulated arrangements.

Using the network is not free, so users only use it for consensus results and if the data are public. You can search the Ethereum Blockchain by visiting the link below:

https://www.etherchain.org/

Even though many examples of these contracts describe different human interactions, the platform is presently used for industrial use-scenarios such as communication between machines or stringent business logic between organizations.

For example, there are power companies that are looking for ways to generate a smarter grid where residences can easily buy power. Another good example is the collaboration between Samsung and IBM for Internet of Things.

Centralized networks are naturally vulnerable because they have one governing platform that could be exposed to an attack. The vision of Ethereum is to decentralize the World Wide Web by building a platform where apps could be created and run on a decentralized hub.

This prevents a single point attack, and if one area is under attack, the rest of the platform is still functional. Therefore, Ethereum is also regarded as the computer of the world, because it has the capacity for decentralizing worldwide networks and so wields unlimited power.

Prior to the development of Ethereum, Blockchain apps were created to perform very specific operations, which is quite problematic for developers. They may choose to either stretch the set of functions provided by Bitcoin or any other form of app (that is time-consuming and could be extremely difficult) or create a new Blockchain app as well as a completely new platform.

Instead of building a completely new Blockchain for every application, Ethereum allows the development of any application within the network. This really makes the Ethereum stand out from the rest of the Blockchains. It also offers the uniterceptable nature of digital currencies such as Bitcoin and stretches it to almost any app that you could think of.

This is the main reason why many experts in cryptocurrency believe that Ethereum will surpass Bitcoin as the top Blockchain, and so believed to be a hot commodity for traders and speculators.

Ethereum is planned at different stages. At present, the Ethereum project is on its second stage known as the Homestead. The four planned stages of Ethereum growth are the following:

Frontier

This stage was the initial introduction of Ethereum in 2015. This was mostly a prototype release to open the platform to more technically skilled programmers to build their own applications, initiate early mining, and start exchanges.

Homestead

Ethereum is currently on this stage. There were some changes compared to the initial plans such as the block incentive was fixed to 5 ether. In the improved Homestead, the platform becomes more of a patchwork of corrections to get rid of the risk warning that you can see on the homepage of Ethereum.

Metropolis

In this stage, the platform will be opened to the public, and the interfaces are fully tested for non-technical participants. Even though this is now being performed by individuals using the Ethereum desktop wallet. There is no definite date for this release and whether it will depend on the pace of the community.

Serenity

This is the last stage of Ethereum project and it highlights one main principle – to transform the Ethereum network from proof-of-work platform to a proof-of-stake platform, which will significantly decrease the power consumption of the Ethereum network. There is no set date for the release although experts believe this will happen in 2018.

Although the Ethereum price has already significantly risen in 2017, there is still potential to see a huge increase to as much as 100 times the present levels.

The financial world also takes a lot of advantage in using a controllable ledger, but it is a bit dubious of its privacy features. Hence, companies have made some innovation to offer Ethereum with their services to aid banks to create their own private networks.

The Ethereum network uses smart contracts, which is a phrased used to describe the code that executes the trade of money, property, content, share, or anything valuable.

When performed on the Blockchain, a smart contract will behave like an automated computer program that immediately runs the code if certain conditions are present. Because smart contracts are running on the Blockchain, they are exactly running as designed without any form of downtime, censorship, interference, or fraud.

In essence, Blockchains are designed to process code, which is mostly limited. This is not the case with Ethereum. Instead of providing a set of restricted operations, developers are free to create any operation they want inside the Ethereum network. Therefore, you can create various applications that are designed to meet specific needs.

Prior to Ethereum, the applications in Blockchains were programmed to perform a very limited set of operations.

For instance, Bitcoin was designed specifically for P2P cash transactions. Many developers experienced problems with this setup.

They may either stretch the set of functions provided by Bitcoin and other forms of applications, which is time-consuming and can be very complicated or design a new application in the Blockchain as well as a completely new platform. With this challenge, the creator of Ethereum, Vitalik Buterin, created a new platform.

The Ethereum Virtual Machine or EVM is a core innovation of the platform. It is a Turing complete software, which runs on the network and enables anyone to run any application regardless of the language used as long as there is enough memory and time in the network.

The EVM facilitates easier and more efficient processing of creating applications in the Blockchain. Rather than creating a completely new Blockchain for every new application, Ethereum allows the creation of various applications in a single platform.

Through Ethereum, developers can create and use decentralized applications with specific functions. For instance, Bitcoin is a program that allows users to transfer digital cash from one user to another. As decentralized applications are built on codes that are running the Blockchain platform, these are not subject to any central authority.

Any centralized service could be converted into a centralized platform through Ethereum. Just consider all the intermediary services that now exist across different areas including banking services, voting systems, title registries, regulatory licensing systems, and much more.

Ethereum is also currently used to create Decentralized Autonomous Organizations or DAO, which are completely decentralized and autonomous organization with no single leading entity. DAOs are running through codes, on a group of smart contracts designed inside the Blockchain used by Ethereum.

The code is written as an alternative to the structure and rules of a conventional organization, which discards the need for people and centralized control. Everyone can own a DAO by purchasing Ethereum tokens. But rather of each token being equivalent to shares and ownership, these tokens serve as contributions that provide people rights to vote.

Since decentralized applications are running on a Blockchain inside Ethereum, they can also take advantage of its properties such as zero downtime, security, risk-free, and immutability. But like other forms of Blockchains and cryptocurrencies, Ethereum and Ether also have their flaws. Although automated and digital in nature, smart contracts are still designed by humans.

Hence, these contracts are only as good as the people who designed them. Oversights and code bugs could also result in unexpected adverse effects. If there is an error in the code, the platform might be exploited, and there are very few ways to stop an attack, which involves getting the consensus of the whole network users and re-programming the core code.

The primary goal of the Ethereum network is to decentralize the World Wide Web. And arguably, it has now achieved some success of becoming the new internet platform. Ethereum has a lot of potential to become an alternative platform for hosting and executing code online.

At present, the market cap of Ethereum is around $ 17 Billion, while the market capitalization of Bitcoin is at $ 34 Billion. Hence, Ether is regarded as the second most valuable digital currency today. This number is projected to rise in a span of a few more years.

Litecoin (LTC)

Introduced in 2011, Litecoin is another type of cryptocurrency that is also based on the Bitcoin platform. This digital currency is created by Charlie Lee, a former engineer at Google and graduate of MIT.

Lee created this cryptocurrency as an open source payment platform that is also free from any interference or governance of a single authority. However, Litecoin is different from Bitcoin in areas such as using scrypt as a proof of work system and it offers faster block generation.

Litecoin was designed as a lower scale currency of Bitcoin. If Bitcoin is gold, then Litecoin is silver. It was created with the objective to improve the shortcomings of the Bitcoin network, and it has already gained support in various industries. Through the years, this digital currency has achieved liquidity and trade volume.

Litecoin production is faster than Bitcoin, specifically four times faster. In general, Litecoin is now one of the top cryptocurrencies in terms of value, but they are easier to obtain compared to most digital currencies.

Similar to other digital currencies, Litecoin also serves as an online cash system. Similar to a bank's online network or PayPal, users could use the network to transfer one currency to another. But rather than US dollars, it performs the transactions in Litecoin units. This is where the similarity of Litecoin ends.

Likewise, Litecoin is also not issued by a government. Rather than being governed by a Federal Reserve and being printed by the government, Litecoins are produced through mining as well similar to Bitcoin mining. Litecoin supply is also fixed currently at 84 million. The Litecoin network creates a block every 2.5 minutes, which is faster compared to the 10 minutes for Bitcoin.

The Litecoin block also refers to the ledger record of recent Litecoin transactions. The block is also confirmed using mining software and made accessible to any user who likes to see the block. When the miner confirms the transaction, the next block will be added to the chain.

The first user to confirm the block will receive 50 Litecoins, which is valued around $ 100. The amount of Litecoins awarded for this task decreases over time. This decreasing rate will continue at regular intervals until all miners confirmed all the 84 million Litecoins.

Mining digital currencies at a rate that is profitable for you requires super processing power, which could be done only if you have specialized software and hardware.

To mine digital currencies, the computational power of your desktop PC is not fast enough for currency mining. This brings us to another benefit of mining Litecoin as it can be mined using regular PCs. You can also mine well if your tools are high-grade.

You should take note that any currency, even the strongest ones, is only worthy if the society deems it valuable. If the Federal Reserve begins circulating too many dollars, its value will decrease. Anything that becomes cheaply available becomes less valuable.

The developers of Litecoin are well aware of this from the very start and they understood that it can be difficult for a new digital currency to gain a reputation in the growing marketplace. But by limiting the number of Litecoins that are in circulation, the developers can at least minimize the fears of people on overproduction.

As we have already mentioned, Litecoin is modeled after the Bitcoin network. Hence, the way to get Litecoins is, to begin with, a Bitcoin account, then trade BTCs for LTCs. The current exchange rate of BTC to LTC is 146 to 1. You might be thinking about the possible benefit of trading a cryptocurrency to a less popular one.

There are several advantages that are inherent to Litecoin, which makes it attractive to use the newer digital currency. Primarily, Litecoin can process more transactions, mainly because of the shorter time for generating a block.

Litecoin also has a lot cheaper transaction fee, posted at 1/1000 of a Litecoin no matter what the volume of the transaction. At the current exchange rate, this is only about

2 cents, which is a lot cheaper compared to the 3% fee on PayPal.

In the actual world, the most dependable stores of value are the currencies of choice during a crisis. For example, Zimbabwe faced hyperinflation starting in the 1990s that wiped out the fortunes of many people.

The currency became the least valuable currency in the world in which Z$ Trillion was only equivalent to 40 cents in US dollars. People had to use more stable currencies such as US dollars, Chinese Yuan, Japanese Yen, and South African Rand for their everyday purchases. The inherent scarcity of Litecoin prevents hyperinflation. The main challenge at the present is to gain widespread use.

When a currency achieves a significant volume of users who agree that the currency is valuable, it will result in stability and sustainability. Litecoin is not yet widely accepted, as there are only fewer than 100,000 current users today. However, as digital currencies become more widely accepted and their values become stable, they will become the currencies of the future.

Ripple (XRP)

Introduced in 2012, Ripple is a real-time worldwide settlement network, which provides affordable overseas payments. This digital currency allows banks to complete international payments in real-time at a fraction of a cost and transparency. With a market capitalization around $ 1.26 billion, Ripple is one of the most valuable digital currencies today.

Similar to Bitcoin and Litecoin, Ripple also maintains a Blockchain known as a consensus ledger as its method of confirmation. However, it does not require mining so it decreases the need to use the computational power and also lessen network latency.

The developers of Ripple believes that value distribution is a great way to incentivize specific behaviors and so they are now distributing the currency mainly via business development deals, offering XRP to organizational buyers who are interested to invest in the currency, and as rewards to providers of liquidity who provide tighter payment spreads.

Even though it was only introduced in 2012, Ripple is actually older than Bitcoin. The project was actually implemented in 2004 by Ryan Fugger who envisioned it as a decentralized monetary system that can effectively empower individuals and organizations in generating their own money.

Basically, Ripple is represented as debt. The transactions are simply composed of balances being transformed on a series of digital cash reserves from one user to another. Let us consider a simple example to explain how Ripple works in practice.

Let us say that there are two friends, Beatrice and Claire who starts road journey. They have decided to bring their own friends. Beatrice brought her cousin Amanda, while Claire invited her friend Donna. Amanda knows Beatrice, but has never met Claire and Donna before. Likewise, Donna has never met Amanda and Beatrice. Let's say that Amanda and Donna want to buy coffee, but Donna doesn't have cash.

So Amanda pays for her coffee at $2 per cup, and Donna promises to pay Amanda back using Ripple. Because it makes no sense to have Donna owe $2 to Amanda, as she may well never have the chance to pay back, she instead agrees to owe $2 to Claire. Claire agrees to owe $2 to Beatrice and Beatrice agrees to owe $2 to Amanda.

Let us assume that Beatrice has an outstanding debt of $1 to Claire prior to the meeting. In this scenario, the debt will be canceled and Claire now only has $1 debt to Beatrice. The main point here is that all debts are between people who have chosen to establish a trust relationship or in financial jargon a credit line.

Hence, they trust each other that they will pay the debt when one party requires money. Through this system, cash could revolve around even between people who don't know each other.

In some areas, this system is actually similar to the way our banking system already works today. Overseas money transfers are collected by banks, cash transfers between banks are canceled out, and then when a bank releases more money compared to what it takes, the banks will replenish cash through different systems designed for this purpose.

The original Ripple project aims to achieve a democratization of this system, so anyone can serve as a bank - capable of receiving and serving as a channel for loans.

The original Ripple project achieves some level of success, and the system can still be accessed on villages.cc and classic.ripplpay.com. But these communities who are using the classic Ripple were far from becoming universal as they never extended beyond the small communities.

This is mainly due to the simple reason that before anyone can join the network, he or she should already have a friend within the network. Or else, there is no way to build a chain of cash reserves between you and other users, so completing a transaction can be impossible.

Another flaw is the centralized software. Even though Fugger aims to create a cash system that was distributed and anyone can participate, the network that monitors all the cash lines and balances must still be controlled in a central hub.

Today, the Ripple network has been improved. The issue in isolated communities is now addressed in two ways: a gateway system and a specialized Ripple currency. The latter is not debt-based unlike other things stored in the network. Hence, the currency could be sent from one user to another just like other digital currencies.

It is now possible to send money to someone who is not part of your local trust network. You just need to convert the currency into XRP, send over the network, which will convert it back. Ripple's built-in decentralized exchange hub converts the currency, so there is now way for users to back off from the deal, as the transaction is recorded into the ledger simultaneously.

Another significant development in the improved Ripple system are the integration of gateways, which are basically a commercial service that serves the role of being a credit middle channel for those who are not yet in the network or possibly those who are not yet connected through someone they know in the network and prefers to use the commercial service.

The gateway will serve as the first layer of the link in the trust chain between the user and the recipient when the user likes to complete a payment, as well as the last link when the user likes to receive money. You can trust several gateways simultaneously, so the network will still maintain a decentralized approach, which is comparable to mining hubs.

Anyone can become a gateway in the Ripple network, which provides a long continuum of network topologies that range from a model of a centralized banking system to a P2P cash system.

During the initial stages, the creators of Ripple believe that gateways will emerge as the norm. But with the growth and success of Ripple, it could happen that as the system gets enough market share, a peer to peer system will eventually rise.

Like in other digital currency platforms, the Ripple gateways are not completely unflawed. Primarily, there is no inherent system to make certain that the gateways will not default on its debts. Also, those who have been using digital currencies such as Bitcoin and Litecoin, are not completely convinced of using a network that needs trust in third-party organizations for its functions.

At this point, Ripple developers are still not offering solutions for these concerns. The Ripple network does not offer a solid solution to this problem, and controlling fraudulent gateways should be done by more conventional mechanisms.

Decentralization is the other primary aspect of Ripple. In essence, the mechanism of Ripple is to monitor the balances, which is pretty much the same as Bitcoin. The Blockchain used by Ripple also uses public and private keys, addresses, and changes to the database are also performed via a system of digitally signed transactions.

As a matter of fact, Ripple uses exactly the same specifications as Bitcoins aside from the primary byte in the address format. Hence, anyone can use the same keys to verify transactions and messages in the Ripple and Bitcoin networks. But instead of mining, the transactions in Ripple are basically propagated via the network, and a given set of contradictory transactions.

For instance, let's say that a fraudulent user initiating transactions to send the same $50 to five various merchants with the hope of receiving $250 worth of goods. The clients should verify first which one received the payment first, and if unverified will be marked as illegitimate, via a process called consensus.

In general, Consensus is an improved platform that is already being used in Bitcoin network for transactions requiring no confirmations. Private nodes decide what version of a new ledger should be accepted through a poll to see the opinion of the majority, which allows the system to easily settle on one choice only.

This process is a bit faster compared to the block confirmation in Bitcoin where a new ledger state is generated about five to 10 seconds, which allow for nearly automatic verification.

Other digital currencies that you might be interested to learn about are Dash, Manero, Altcoins, and much more.

7 - How to Make Money in Cryptocurrency

There are strong indications that digital currencies will become widely accepted in the near future. And similar to fiat currencies that most of us use today, you can harness the benefits of cryptocurrencies in order to make money.

In this Chapter, we will discuss the recommended methods that you can try to make money in specific cryptocurrencies.

Bitcoin Mining

We have already discussed how Bitcoin mining works earlier in this book, so in this section, we will provide you the technical and strategic details on how you can make money through mining Bitcoins.

Basically, Bitcoin miners are not people, because the actual mining is performed by a hardware, essentially a supercomputer used to execute the sophisticated mathematical computations needed to encrypt and decrypt processes on the network.

For the sake of discussion, we will refer to this hardware as miners or Bitcoin miners, while those who are running the hardware will be called ledger managers or Bitcoin ledger managers.

After mining for Bitcoins for some time, you will learn that this activity is highly technical, so in the part of a ledger manager, it can be an easy task because you really don't need to do anything. However, it really involves sophisticated algorithms and tons of math.

But it is not necessary to master these computations before you can make money from mining. Rather, we will only discuss the important things for you to begin with Bitcoin mining and determine if you can really make some profit.

Bitcoin was developed to prevent any type of centralized regulation, similar to governments and banks have over fiat currencies. This is what makes the cryptocurrency unique, and this is also what provides Bitcoin its advantage as a currency.

In order for the Bitcoin system to work, without outside interference, miners play an important role in maintaining the Blockchain and monitor all transactions on the network.

Every time a transaction happens, all miners verify their ledgers and adjust the chain accordingly.

Bitcoin mining is actually a numbers game, where everyone has a number, each transaction has a number, and every Bitcoin has a number. As a matter of fact, it is more accurate to say that everything in a Bitcoin is a number instead of has a number.

Every time that there is a transaction, the system will generate a number, and Bitcoin miners will work to confirm the transaction by decoding the encryption.

How to Get Started in Bitcoin Mining

Before you can make money in Bitcoin mining, you should first invest in the recommended hardware. And just a heads up, it can be expensive. You might need to spend a few thousand dollars if you want to keep up with the growing user base and demand in the Bitcoin network.

For example, one suggested hardware is the ASIC Bitcoin miner Antminer S7 28nm, which costs around $ 2,600. But there are still miners that only cost for as low as $400.

During the early years of Bitcoin, ledger managers began with regular PCs that are only used for Bitcoin mining. With the rise of Bitcoin as a digital currency, mining called for higher computational power. For as short as one year, ledger managers used PCs installed with a special card designed solely for Bitcoin mining. Since then, more sophisticated Bitcoin miners have been introduced.

It is important to take note that being a ledger manager requires continuous investment as with the projected widespread use of Bitcoin, more and more ledger managers will participate in the network, and as a result, better ways will be eventually developed.

On average, new Bitcoin miners are developed at least once a year, but there is no guarantee. Apart from the Bitcoin miner, you also have to use a specific power supply, which may range from $ 60 to $ 800, and even more depending on the requirements by the miner.

Aside from the cost of the mining tools, you also need to consider the power cost. Bitcoin miners consume some electricity, so you have to factor in this cost. For instance, if you are paying around 20 cents for every kilowatt, one Bitcoin miner may cost you about $ 6 every day.

But if you are running the right hardware, and you are living in an area where power is affordable, then you only need to consider a few dollars each day.

The cost of power for every kilowatt is varying from one state to another. So far, the east coast has the highest cost, with as high as 15 cents per kilowatt in Florida. Be sure to consider this as it can be useless to go for Bitcoin mining if the cost is higher than what you can earn. But how much money can you make in Bitcoin mining?

The Bitcoin network is designed to integrate blocks of transactions for every 10 minutes. Hence, you can't decrypt every transaction as they are made. Your hardware has to perform this in blocks.

Every block is worth around 25 BTCs. However, the price of the actual coin will depend on the present conversion rate of Bitcoin, which will vary from day to day. As of this writing, 1 BTC is equivalent to $ 2,749.94. Hence, for every block, you can solve or verify, you can earn a total of $ 68,748.50.

There are two methods you can try to earn money through

Bitcoin mining: solo mining and pool mining.

As the name suggests, solo mining refers to the lone strategy of mining on your own. You set up all the needed hardware. Then you play the race of decrypting a block before other miners succeed.

The second method is known as pool mining, in which you participate in a group of ledger managers who are coordinating with each other for decoding the blocks. For every block that your group solves, you share in the payment, depending on how much work your hardware allocated.

You might need around $ 3,000 to $ 5,000 to get started in Bitcoin Mining. Many ledger managers are using several miners to increase their odds of solving the blocks first.

Other Ways of Making Money in Bitcoin

Mining is not the only way to make money in the Bitcoin market. You could also try speculation trading in the stock markets or by trading Bitcoins. In 2010, the cost of Bitcoin was only $12 per coin.

Seven years later, its price skyrocketed to $2,749.94. You

could have been a millionaire if you purchased $ 5,000 worth of Bitcoins in 2010. But of course, there is always the risk of volatility, as trading Bitcoin has the same inherent risk in the stock market.

It takes time to learn how you can invest in stocks through Bitcoin. There are several ETF, which trades on Bitcoin depending on the movement of the price. This has similar mechanism in investing in gold ETF.

One company may purchase the commodity or invests in companies that depend on this commodity then sell the share of the company. You actually don't have ownership of the coins, but your stocks move alongside the commodity price.

Becoming an exchanger is possibly the easiest way to make a profit through Bitcoin trading. You just need to sign up with a P2P exchange marketplace such as LocalBitcoins or BitSquare, then you can start offering an exchange service in a local area for buying and selling Bitcoins.

Adding a spread will allow you to make some profit. For instance, a buy offer for 2 per cent below market price and sell offer for 2 per cent above the selling price. People are usually happy with this spread if you can provide easy ways for anyone to trade Bitcoins.

However, you should be aware that you might probably need to secure some deals first by responding to other people's ads and then shouldering the cost of the initial spread so you can start getting a good reputation in the industry

You don't really need to become a master in financial analysis before you can become a Bitcoin exchanger. This is the reason why it is easy for this to start. Becoming a digital currency trader requires more skill and knowledge. As a trader, you may need to use online exchanges and you can purchase or sell depending on whether the people will believe the price will fall or rise.

You can also provide a service of filling up order books, which could be taken up by individuals who want to trade for more practical reasons. However, your focus may not be on offering a service to customers, providing great customer service, or nurturing relationships. Your focus could simply on getting offers as a form of guessing game if the market will rise or fall.

If you are interested to become a Bitcoin trader, providing P2P exchange service could be an ideal way to begin. As long as the market doesn't fluctuate that much, it can be possible for the trader to make more profit regardless of the price movement.

But simultaneously, if the market follows an upward trend, then it is recommended to purchase more. Hence, a Bitcoin exchanger can also make more profit by becoming a Bitcoin trader while providing exchange services for those who are not yet decided to become a trader to minimize the risk and also to test the waters.

Even with exchanges done on a centralized hub, where you don't usually deal with your customers, you can still make profits by providing exchange services. You can do this by creating instead of taking offers. When you place offers into the orderbooks instead of accepting offers that are already there, you can possibly gain a better price.

Since you are also offering a service, you also serve the role of being the market maker who enables the exchange center to serve as an exchanger even without the large capital. Most exchanges will also provide you some rewards to motivate you to become a maker instead of being a taker. This could come in the form of decreased trading fees, zero trading fees, or even rewards and bonuses.

Top Strategies for Bitcoin Trading

A well-defined and clear strategy will increase your chances of success in Bitcoin trading. You have to know precisely what you like when you are opening a trade, how much profit you like prior to building up before you can take the offer, your loss tolerance, and much more. You have to clearly identify what timescale you are looking at and what forms of changes will make you rethink your strategy.

Monitoring the Trend

Financial markets usually have long-term price trends, in which the general movement follows a single direction for months and even years. There are some minor fluctuations, but in general, the trend will remain clear.

Some traders in digital currencies will just look for this long-term trend and trade in this direction. There is even no need to identify the point at which a trend would turn and a new one starts in the opposing direction, as long as you don't need to make a withdrawal anytime soon.

When an average trend requires around a year to complete, then it is really pointless if it may take you six months to be sure that it is a new trend.

Technical Analysis

Technical Analysis involves the use of chart patterns and mathematical formulae to project the future direction of price movement. This analysis is completely based on the past price data and possibly volume data. Hence, it says nothing about if the price is too low or too high objectively. Instead, you have to determine if there are particular recurring trends and patterns that will soon appear on the market.

Most of these are heavily postulated on human psychology – the notion that people just need to act in a specific way to different movement in prices. Some traders also believe that changes in the real underlying value are already priced by participants in the market, and so taking a closer look at the actions of the people in the market can provide you a hint and guide your decision for trading.

Fundamental Analysis

If you are into the stock market, you will surely be familiar with fundamental analysis, which you can also use as a recommended strategy for trading bitcoins.

In this strategy, you have to look at the fundamental information that may affect the price of a digital currency such as a number of coins traded on exchange centers, number of active digital wallets versus the number of digital wallets, number of cryptocurrency transactions every day, and much more.

You can then use this data to project what you believe Bitcoin will be worth at the moment, then decide if you think it is presently overvalued or undervalued, and then trade according to your assessment.

News Watch

Market price will usually rise or fall depending on what is on the news. For instance, the news of Bitcoin website being hacked or an announcement from the government that it will start regulating cryptocurrencies might result to a price down, while new funding for new startups or large companies accepting cryptocurrencies will cause the price to rise.

Trading cryptocurrencies based on news alone is not an ideal strategy, as it can be difficult to always read the news first and respond accordingly.

More often than not, the market might already have made some movement before you can even act – even though if you have the time to always read the news or you have set up an app to send you instant notifications on relevant news, then you might be able to get there first.

Another approach is to leverage on corrections. Usually, the market over reacts to significant news stories as people could jump on or get caught in the moment, without really thinking through it. For example, a 15% fall is usually immediately followed by a 5% increase as the market may rectify this over reaction. This is another opportunity for you to leverage the news and make some profit.

Swing Trade

The methods described above are strategies for the medium or long term. You may need to wait several months or years before you can build a good return for your efforts, and there is always the possibility to end up making small profits or take losses for many months.

Day trading is a faster-paced approach to make money. This strategy refers to the buying and selling Bitcoins based on the short-term movements in the price, usually over the course of hours or days instead of months or years.

Swing Trading is the most common strategy for day trading. This approach utilized a range of technical indicators to search for the turning points in trends at short-term. You can make a profit from the daily swings depending on the fluctuations of the price of the digital currency regardless of whether the long-term movement is rising or falling.

This usually involves searching for resistance and support levels. A resistance level refers to the rising price movement where traders are expected to resist the sellers taking a profit, while a support level refers to the falling price level where buyers are expected to resist into the market to gain from an expected bargain.

Take note that the Bitcoin market has high volatility, which means each part of it relies on something else that makes it quite impossible to know what to do when it comes to making a profit.

Factor in the added work of setting up the hardware, as well as solving maintenance needs, it can be said that Bitcoin mining requires passion and enthusiasm. You need money to make money so you have to invest in the recommended hardware. In addition, you might be at a significant disadvantage if you are not that technically savvy. Also, don't expect a stable income from Bitcoin mining.

Arguably, Bitcoin mining is not the best way to make money online, considering the sheer number of challenges you have to overcome. But this is the reason why the rewards are hefty, as not everyone can do it.

How to Make Money with Ethereum

At its current phase, Ethereum is just similar Bitcoin when it was first released in 2009. There was even this story about a man purchasing Bitcoins worth $27 in 2009, but then forgot about it. Year after he discovered that the value ballooned to $ 980,000. Hence, people are excited about Ethereum as it is poised to become the next Bitcoin or even surpass the digital currency.

There are great indicators suggesting that buying Ethereum is good for long-term investments.

Primarily, the technology used in building the Ethereum network can be used for several purposes. Hence, it is a breakthrough technology with the capacity to affect many industries. In addition, the value of Ethereum as a digital currency will continue to rise as the demand for the platform and its smart contracts continue to rise.

When it comes to stability, Ethereum shows an organic growth without large spikes, and it indicates predictability and stability. The rising value and demand of a specific cryptocurrency are a good sign of its potential. Regardless of the reason, it still increases the demand, which will affect the current price of Ethereum.

Ethereum also starts to create waves in the established industry. Teams from MIT are now conducting active research on Ethereum, while IBM and Microsoft are also offering Ethereum as a Blockchain service. The design of Ethereum as a world computer has enticed significant individuals such as Bill Gates.

Where and How to Buy Ethereum?

There are different platforms online where you can buy Ethereum such as Coinbase, which serves like a digital wallet. This is available to users in more than 30 countries such as United States, Canada, Singapore, United Kingdom, Belgium, Croatia, Denmark, France, Hungary, Italy, Malta, Norway, Netherlands, Poland, Spain, Switzerland, Sweden, and more.

Today, Coinbase is the largest broker of digital currencies where you can purchase Ethereum and Bitcoin with a linked bank account, Interac Online, SEPA transfer, and other common payment methods.

The Coinbase dashboard is quite user-friendly, and easy for new users to trade Ethereum and Bitcoin. Moreover, it is easy to purchase cryptocurrencies using your debit card or credit card.

Coinbase headquarters is located in San Francisco and funded by the biggest investors in fintech today, so it is pretty much a reliable platform.

The first step that you have to do is to register for a Coinbase account, which will provide you a secure place to keep your Ethereum as well as easy payment methods to transform your local currency into Bitcoin or Ethereum. Currently, when you register for a Coinbase account, you can get free $10 worth of Bitcoin if you trade $ 100 worth of Bitcoins.

The next step is to link your accounts such as debit card, credit card, or bank account. You also have to finish some confirmation steps prior to using your Coinbase account. When you complete the verification steps, you can now start trading Ethereum or Bitcoin.

After initiating your first purchase, the network will fulfill your order and deliver your purchased currencies. Take note that the price of Ether changes every day, so the dashboard will show you the prevailing exchange rate before you purchase.

At present, Ether is priced high in the market, and there is still the possibility to increase up to 100 times its current value.

Ethereum Mining

Mining for Bitcoin began with basic bare and bones GPU and CPU mining, which could be performed on high-powered PCs prior to the development of ASIC miners that caused the introduction of specialized hardware. However, the Blockchain used by Ethereum is a lot more resistant to these miners, which has expedited the processing even with using only GPUs.

If you are using a high-powered gaming system, then you already have a hardware that is capable enough for Ether mining. While you can mine Ethereum as an individual, you can still gain better results by working in a pool.

However, you should still consider the increasing challenge associated to a price hike. Ether is at an all-time high price today, but it can be pointless to mine if power costs are now so high. Moreover, the developers of Ethereum have arguably a neutral view when it comes to mining.

As a result, about 90 per cent of all miners for the Bitcoin Blockchain are from China, which causes considerable political strife as well as a lack of innovation. The developers of Ethereum are well aware of this and so they are trying to come up with a solution.

At this point, it may not be the best idea to invest heavily in equipment for mining Ethereum as it could be difficult for you to become profitable in the long-term.

8 - The Future of Cryptocurrency

We may still wait for a decade before any state government official recognizes Bitcoin or any other digital currency as a preferred currency. Just recently, Bitcoin experienced 35% price fluctuation after the US government denied the proposal of the Winklevos Bitcoin Trust for exchange trading.

The US Securities and Exchange Commissioned denied the said proposal mainly because of concerns that Bitcoin might be used for illegal purposes such as drugs trade, terrorism funding, and black market trading. But there is still hope and in the next few years, we might see some significant progress for alternative currencies we have.

While Bitcoin experienced some price drop, a more affordable cryptocurrency – Ether – has recently reached its all-time high price. Even though the current setup of Ether prevents you from using it for direct payment, digital currencies in general still seem to have a brighter future because of new innovations such as smart contracts.

Furthermore, more privacy-focused digital currency alternatives are beginning to gain popularity in favor of platforms like Bitcoin that in spite of their tight security measures, still has some loopholes that could be taken advantage for personal data.

Another exciting news is the acceptance of Bitcoin in academic organizations pioneered by the University of Ohio in their Bitcoin classes as an integral part of its MFE curriculum. Other colleges in the US are also now accepting Bitcoins, which is a significant progress in the journey of cryptocurrencies in the mainstream.

In general, this acceptance of Bitcoin has already resulted in several companies considering large investment opportunities in cryptocurrency, which further fuels its destiny to become mainstream.

It might be too early to say that digital currencies will become the norm, but now we are certain that they are gaining popularity as we progress into a new age.

Why Cryptocurrencies Are Seen As Dangerous Innovation?

Financial organizations around the world have mixed response to the existence of self-regulating cryptocurrencies that are now gradually gaining popularity. Most banks are now reviewing their business model, specifically trying to search for answers on how digital currencies will affect their business.

However, some banking experts suggest that digital currencies can, in fact, be used by banks to underscore the security of conventional banking systems versus Blockchain technologies.

We now regularly read news reports about the volatility of cryptocurrencies like Bitcoin and Ether, because of the unstable and variable trading value in the previous years.

Even though these digital currencies are on their all-time high, it is still worthy to take note that in 2013, the value of Bitcoin dramatically dropped from $200 to $60 in only a matter of three months, and then rise again to around $1250 after seven months.

In addition, the low liquidity of Bitcoin also plays an integral part in how it is being embraced in the trading industry, mainly because liquidity usually determines how many partners are open to trade with the commodity. Experts in the financial markets suggest that the low liquidity of cryptocurrencies mean they are now considered as high-risk investment.

Financial experts also suggest that even though there are few ways to minimize the risk of digital currencies at present, Bitcoin traders are usually not influenced by negative news on digital currencies.

Remember, the inherent volatility of Bitcoin is still a high risk for many investors and organizations, and as indicators suggest, there is no great way to hedge this risk. Hence, most brokers and institutions may decide to put off their investment at the moment, and this is just playing safe.

Meanwhile, there are still thousands of individuals and organizations who are investing in Bitcoins, and this suggests that they are putting their trust on the digital currency as a mainstream commodity in the future.

The World Wide Impact of Digital Currencies

Even though the United Kingdom has already announced

its openness to trading digital currencies, China is being hostile to this new cash platform.

At the peak of Bitcoin's popularity in China, its value significantly dropped because of government restrictions and hostility. In 2013, China officially banned financial organizations from trading cryptocurrencies and regulators also thwarted payment organizations from trading Bitcoins. Of course, this has caused detrimental effects on the success of Bitcoin in China.

Before the ban, China was regarded as the largest world market for Bitcoin and its prices were even higher compared to the US and European exchanges. But this all changed when the Chinese government officially opposed the use of cryptocurrencies in Chinese soil.

Even though Bitcoin is still legal in China, it can be very difficult to use because of the restrictions and hostility imposed by the government on individuals and financial organizations. Experts believe that it is a major challenge for Bitcoin in China to be accepted and the government hostility will not likely to change until this focus changes.

Basically, the challenge for digital currencies in China is focused more on mining and speculation instead of genuine acceptance. Take note that the currency's value is dependent on its acceptance and use by the society for exchanging goods or services.

Even though some businesses started to accept Bitcoins as payment in China, the Chinese society, in general, was not focused on cultivating acceptance, but instead feeding and fueling speculation.

Why are some governments like China hostile to digital currencies? Experts believe that on the point of view of a government, cryptocurrencies pose possible risks to the economy of a nation because they will allow people to complete large transactions out from the country without government interference usually in form of tax.

For instance, if regular people can easily buy overseas involving Bitcoins that is worth millions of dollars, the economy might collapse if not at least falter. Regulating the use of Bitcoin today, while still monitoring its worldwide acceptance allows the government to control the risk while still being open to the advantages of cryptocurrencies.

8 - THE FUTURE OF CRYPTOCURRENCY

Most financial organizations and governments around the world are demonstrating a wait and see strategy when it comes to cryptocurrencies. There are few financial experts who believe that cryptocurrencies will be just a fad, so they may just disappear after some years, while others trust in the platform as the future of our payments.

As more and more cryptocurrencies are introduced, there is a higher opportunity for competitors to innovate more platforms that would overtake the top cryptocurrencies today. The future cryptocurrencies could change our current business and societal landscape if they can provide better stability and higher liquidity than Bitcoin.

9 - Conclusion

Thanks again for taking the time to purchase this book!

You should now have a good understanding of cryptocurrencies, and be able to guide your decision whether to use digital currencies or even harness its advantages for you to make money.

Thank You

As we reach the end of this book, I want to say thanks for reading this book.

I want to get this information out to as many people as possible. If you found this book helpful, I would greatly appreciate you leaving me a review. This helps others find the book as well.

Disclaimer

This document is geared towards providing exact and reliable information in regards to the topic and issue covered. The publication is sold on the idea that the publisher is not required to render an accounting, officially permitted, or otherwise, qualified services. If advice is necessary, legal, financial, medical or professional, a practiced individual in the profession should be ordered.

This information is not presented by a financial or medical practitioner and is for entertainment, educational and informational purposes only. The content is not intended as a substitute for professional medical advice, diagnosis, or treatment. Always seek the advice of your physician or other qualified health care provider with any questions you may have regarding a medical condition. Never disregard professional medical advice or delay in seeking it because of something you have read.

The information provided herein is stated to be truthful and consistent, in that any liability, in terms of inattention or otherwise, by any usage or abuse of any policies, processes, or directions contained within is the solitary and utter responsibility of the recipient reader. Under no circumstances

DISCLAIMER

will any legal responsibility or blame be held against the publisher for any reparation, damages, or monetary loss due to the information herein, either directly or indirectly.

Last Updated: 28.Aug.2017